FLANNEL AND TAROT

Amanda M Clarke

Daily Tarot Guidance from
Gen Xer's

Daily Guidance
SERIES

Koru Publishing

KORU (Maori:NZ)
A symbol of spiritual growth and spiritual connection.

Dear Seekers of Gen X wisdom,

Welcome to a tarot experience that isn't wrapped in velvet cloaks or shrouded in mystical mists. "Flannel and Tarot : Daily Tarot Guidance from Gen Xer's" cuts straight through the esoteric fog to deliver tarot readings with a side of nostalgia and a dash of no-nonsense wisdom.

This book is your backdoor pass to a unique blend of spirituality and cultural throwback, designed specifically for those who came of age in the era of grunge and analog. With each page you turn, you'll stumble upon randomly placed tarot cards, inviting you to connect deeply with the spirits of our generation.

Charge the book with your energy, pose your questions, and let the Spirits of Gen X guide you. Whether you're looking for guidance, a reflection on your current path, or just a moment to reminisce, this book is here to serve. Dive in and rediscover the magic of your era.

Warm regards,

Amanda Clarke

Copyright © 2024 by Koru Lifestylist

All rights reserved. All content, materials, and intellectual property in this book or any other platform owned by Koru Lifestylist are protected by copyright laws. This includes text, images, graphics, videos, audio, software, and any other form of content that may be produced by Koru Lifestylist.

No part of this content may be reproduced, distributed, or transmitted in any form or by any means without the prior written permission of Koru Lifestylist. This means that you cannot copy, reproduce, or use any of the content in this book for commercial or personal purposes without the express written consent of Koru Lifestylist.

Unauthorized use of any copyrighted material owned by Koru Lifestylist may result in legal action being taken against you. Koru Lifestylist reserves the right to pursue all available legal remedies against any individual or entity found to be infringing on its copyright.

In summary, Koru Lifestylist © 2024 holds exclusive rights to all the content produced by it, and any unauthorized use of such content will result in legal action.

FLANNEL & TAROT
Daily Tarot Guidance from Gen Xer's

Introduction to Gen X Speak:
Hey, cool cat—welcome to a trip down nostalgia lane with a mystical twist. If you're expecting some lofty, esoteric textbook, you're in the wrong aisle. This book is like your favorite vintage store—full of surprises, no apologies, and definitely no regular rulebook. Remember how we did it back in the day? Mixtapes, underground zines, DIY or die? That's the spirit we're channeling here.

Vibing Your Energy into Your Book:
Before you dive in, you've gotta make this book yours. Hold it in your hands and think back to those heady days—the first concert you went to, the smell of rain on hot pavement, your first epic road trip. Let all those memories and feelings seep into the pages. This book works best when it's fully charged with your personal brand of rebel energy. It's about making a connection, like hooking up your old console and feeling the buzz as it whirs to life.

How to Use This Book:

Using this book is as straightforward as flipping through your old high school yearbook:

1. Set Your Intentions: Think about what you really want to know. Whether it's a burning question about your love life, career moves, or just the daily grind.

2. Call on the Spirits of Gen Xers: Just say it out loud—ask those gritty, grunge-era energies to guide you.

3. Flip It Like a Record: Let your fingers riffle through the pages and stop wherever it feels right. No peeking; let the surprise hit you like the bass at a live show.

4. Read Your Card: The page you land on holds your card and its message. Take it in. What's it saying? Is it a wake-up call, or is it telling you to chill out and watch the reruns?

Journaling:

After you've read your card, go to the journaling pages at the back of this book - You're going to need a HB Pencil, remember them? Scrawl down whatever thoughts came up for you. How does this reading fit into your day? Does it remind you of a song, a movie, or a moment?

The Answers You Seek

Are Within

The Moon

Illusion, fear, anxiety.

Not everything is as it seems. Trust your instincts and don't get lost in illusions or fear.

Quick take...

I GUESS SO!?!

A lot to be said for 'Intuition'. Be aware of the shadows.

Eight of Wands

Speed, action, communication.

Swift action and communication. Get moving and say what needs to be said. No time to waste.

Quick take...

TOTALLY!

OMG... already!
Move fast or come last.

Page of Pentacles

Curiosity, potential, new beginnings.

Eager as a newbie learning the ropes in a new job, this card signifies exploration of new financial opportunities or studies.

Quick take...

GO FOR IT!

You don't want to stay stagnant... keep learning!

Two of Wands

Planning, decisions, direction.

Planning your next big move, like figuring out whether to stay or go on a job offer overseas.

Quick take...

I GUESS SO!?!

Just make a choice already and go for it ... why wait?!?

Seven of Pentacles

Patience, investment, growth.

Patience in growth, like waiting for your favorite band's next album. Good things take time.

Quick take... **MEH ... WHATEVER!**

Go watch the grass grow while you wait!

Two of Cups

Partnership, connection, unity.

Partnerships and connections. Whether it's love or friendship, make it count. It's all about the bond.

Quick take...

TOTALLY!

Bro or Ho code - It no matter. Just get connected and have fun.

Two of Pentacles

Balance, adaptability, multitasking.

Balancing more than one job like a DJ with two turntables. Keep things in motion carefully.

Quick take...

MEH ... WHATEVER!

*Give up the juggling act...
Just get a balanced spin!*

King of Swords

Authority, truth, intellect.

Authority like a seasoned DJ controlling the mix. Fair, strategic, and analytical leadership.

Quick take...

GO FOR IT!

Lead with logic and avoid the tragic.

Two of Swords

Indecision, stalemate, choices.

Decision time, like choosing between watching MTV or VH1. A stalemate needing a new perspective.

Quick take...
MEH ...
WHATEVER!
Decide or get stuck forever.

The Tower

Upheaval, disaster, revelation.

Sudden upheaval, like a surprise album drop that changes everything. It's shocking but clears the way for new structures.

Quick take...

AS IF ... NO WAY!

Kick through the chaos and rebuild anew.

Ten of Pentacles

Wealth, inheritance, family.

Legacy time. Think long-term and build something that lasts. Family matters.

Quick take...

GO FOR IT!

Build a lasting legacy ... abundance for the whole family

Justice

Fairness, justice, truth.

Play fair and keep your integrity intact. Karma's watching, so make sure your actions are just and balanced.

Quick take...
YEP ... FOR SURE!

Balance the scales... truth prevails!

Ace of Pentacles

New beginnings, prosperity, opportunity.

Like landing a first job with a corner office, a new financial or material opportunity arises. Seize it with both hands.

Quick take...

GO FOR IT!

Take the money and run.

Ace of Cups

New love, emotions, beginnings.

New emotions or relationships. Dive in if you want, but don't get too attached. Feel the feels then let it go!

Quick take...

TOTALLY!

Feel it, but don't cling to it.

Ten of Swords

Endings, defeat, collapse.

Feels like the worst series finale ever. Something ends definitively, but it's time to move on.

Quick take...

NOPE... NOT EVEN!

*Rock bottom??
The only way is up, baby!*

The Lovers

Love, union, choices.

A choice in love or dilemma like choosing between two great season finales. Harmony or conflict, it's a pivotal decision.

Quick take...

I GUESS SO!?!

Make a choice and stick to it.

Seven of Cups

Choices, illusions, opportunities.

Choices like video rental stores in the 90s—so many options. Not all are what they seem, so choose wisely.

Quick take...

I GUESS SO!?!

Choose reality over daydreams.

The Magician

Manifestation, resourcefulness, power.

You've got the skills, now use them. Stop overthinking and just get stuff done. Be your own boss.

Quick take...
YEP ... FOR SURE!

Do it yourself, no one's gonna help you.

King of Wands

Leadership, vision, honor.

Like the director of a blockbuster, you're in control of this dynamic project or situation.

Quick take...

TOTALLY!

Be the visionary leader.

Eight of Pentacles

Skill development, hard work.

Work hard, play hard. Perfect your skills and enjoy the grind. Mastery awaits.

Quick take...

GO FOR IT!

Grind now, shine later.

Page of Cups

Creativity, intuition, messages.

Creative ideas and messages. Let your imagination run wild and share your thoughts. Be open.

Quick take...

TOTALLY!

Share your creative vibes.

The Chariot

Victory, willpower, determination.

Keep moving forward, no matter what. Life's a journey with bumps, so buckle up and keep your eyes on the road.

Quick take...

YEP ... FOR SURE!

Keep moving, no matter what.

Wheel of Fortune

Change, cycles, fate.

Life's a rollercoaster, and you're not in control. Go with the flow and don't freak out when things get weird.

Quick take...

I GUESS SO!?!

Ride the wave, don't fight it.

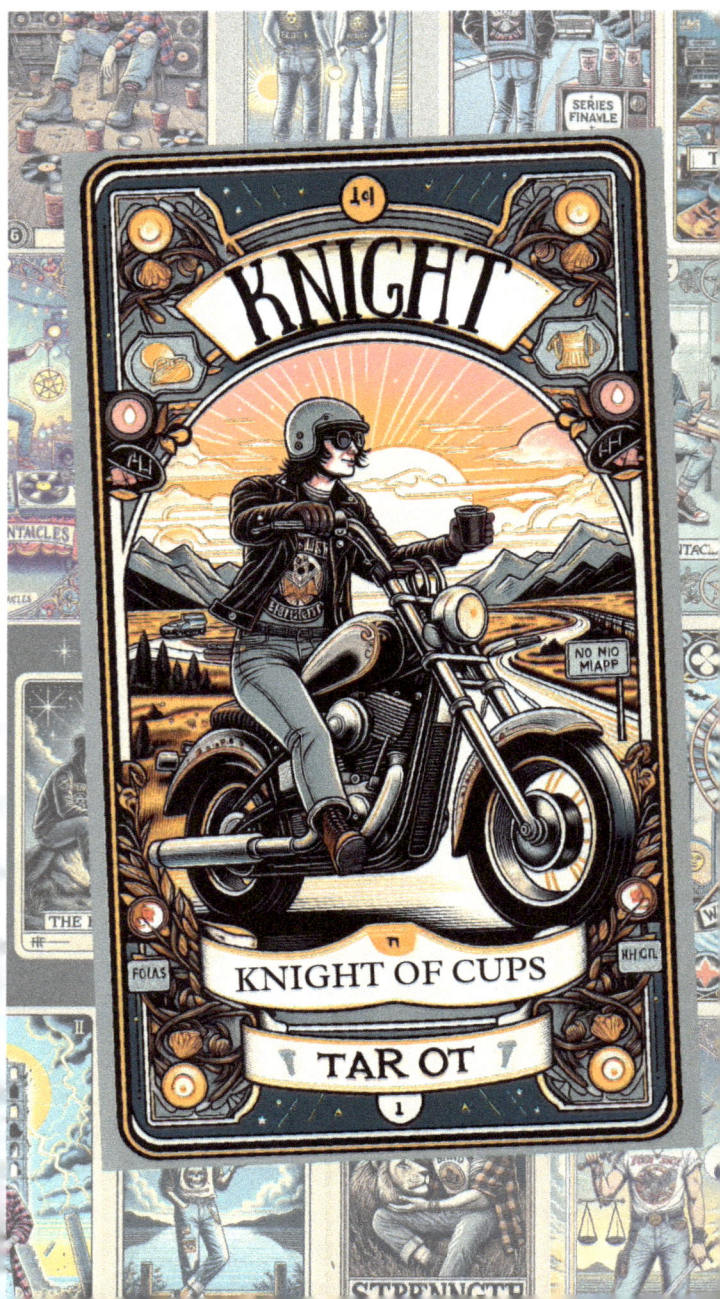

Knight of Cups

Romance, adventure, charm.

Romantic and charming. Go after what you want with style, but don't be a player.

Quick take...

MEH ... WHATEVER!

Charm your way to success.

The Fool

New beginnings, adventure, take risks.

Don't take life too seriously, man. Sometimes you just gotta wing it and see what happens. Don't sweat the small stuff.

Quick take...

I GUESS SO!?!

Whatever, let's just go for it.

Nine of Cups

Satisfaction, contentment, wishes fulfilled.

Wish fulfilled. You got what you wanted, now enjoy it. Don't look a gift horse in the mouth.

Quick take...

TOTALLY!

Enjoy your wishes come true.

Four of Cups

pathy, contemplation, reevaluation.

Feeling like reruns are all that's on TV. Take a moment to see if there's an overlooked opportunity or relationship update.

Quick take...

I GUESS SO!?!

Snap out of your funk.

Nine of Swords

Anxiety, fear, nightmares.

Anxiety like waiting for the dial-up to connect. Overwhelmed by worries, find ways to cope.

Quick take...

NOPE... NOT EVEN!

Suck it up buttercup... Face your fears!

The Empress

Abundance, nurturing, nature.

Enjoy the good things in life but don't get too comfy. Nothing lasts forever, so appreciate the moment.

Quick take...

YEP ... FOR SURE!

Enjoy it now, it won't last forever.

Seven of Wands

Defense, perseverance, challenge.

Defend your position. Hold your ground, but don't be stubborn. Pick your battles.

Quick take...

I GUESS SO!?!

Defend, but choose your battles.

Ace of Wands

Inspiration, new beginnings, potential.

New inspiration or project. Go for it, but don't expect miracles. Just start already.

Quick take...

TOTALLY!

Start now, figure it out later.

The Star

Hope, faith, rejuvenation.

Stay hopeful, even when things suck. Keep dreaming and aiming high. Your time to shine will come.

Quick take...

YEP ... FOR SURE!

Keep the faith, even in the dark.

Ten of Cups

Harmony, happiness, fulfillment.

Happy families and emotional fulfillment. Soak it up and spread the love. Harmony rules.

Quick take...

TOTALLY!

Soak up the love.

Five of Cups

Loss, grief, moving on.

Crying over spilled milk? Move on already. Focus on what you have, not what you lost.

Quick take...

DON'T EVEN GO THERE!

Move on and let it go.

The Sun

Joy, success, positivity.

Soak up the good vibes and enjoy life. Shine bright and spread positivity. Life's too short to be miserable.

Quick take...

YEP ... FOR SURE!

Enjoy life, spread good vibes.

Temperance

Balance, moderation, purpose.

Find your balance and chill out. Moderation in everything keeps the peace. Don't go overboard.

Quick take...

I GUESS SO!?!

Stay balanced, avoid extremes.

Three of Wands

Expansion, foresight, progress.

Looking ahead and waiting. Patience, dude. Your ships will come in, eventually.

Quick take...

TOTALLY!

Patience, your time will come.

Knight of Wands

Passion, adventure, impulsiveness.

Passion and impulsiveness. Chase your dreams but don't crash and burn. Balance the fire.

Quick take...

TOTALLY!

Chase dreams, avoid burnout.

Nine of Wands

Resilience, persistence, courage.

Resilience and perseverance. Keep going, even when it sucks. You're almost there.

Quick take...

I GUESS SO!?!

Persevere through the pain.

Five of Wands

Conflict, competition, challenges.

Conflict and competition. Stand your ground but don't be a jerk. Play fair.

Quick take...

I GUESS SO!?!

Stand your ground, play fair.

Five of Swords

Conflict, betrayal, defeat.

Winning at all costs leaves you alone. Think about what really matters.

Quick take...

NOPE... NOT EVEN!

Winning isn't everything.

The High Priestess

Intuition, mystery, subconscious.

Trust your gut. You already know what's up, just tune out the noise and listen to your intuition.

Quick take...

I GUESS SO!?!

Shut up and listen to your inner voice.

Eight of Swords

Restriction, limitation, fear.

Feeling trapped? It's all in your head. Break free from the mental chains.

Quick take...

NOPE... NOT EVEN!

Free your mind.

Seven of Swords

Deception, trickery, strategy.

Sneaky tactics get you nowhere. Be honest or face the fallout.

Quick take...

NOPE... NOT EVEN!

Honesty over trickery.

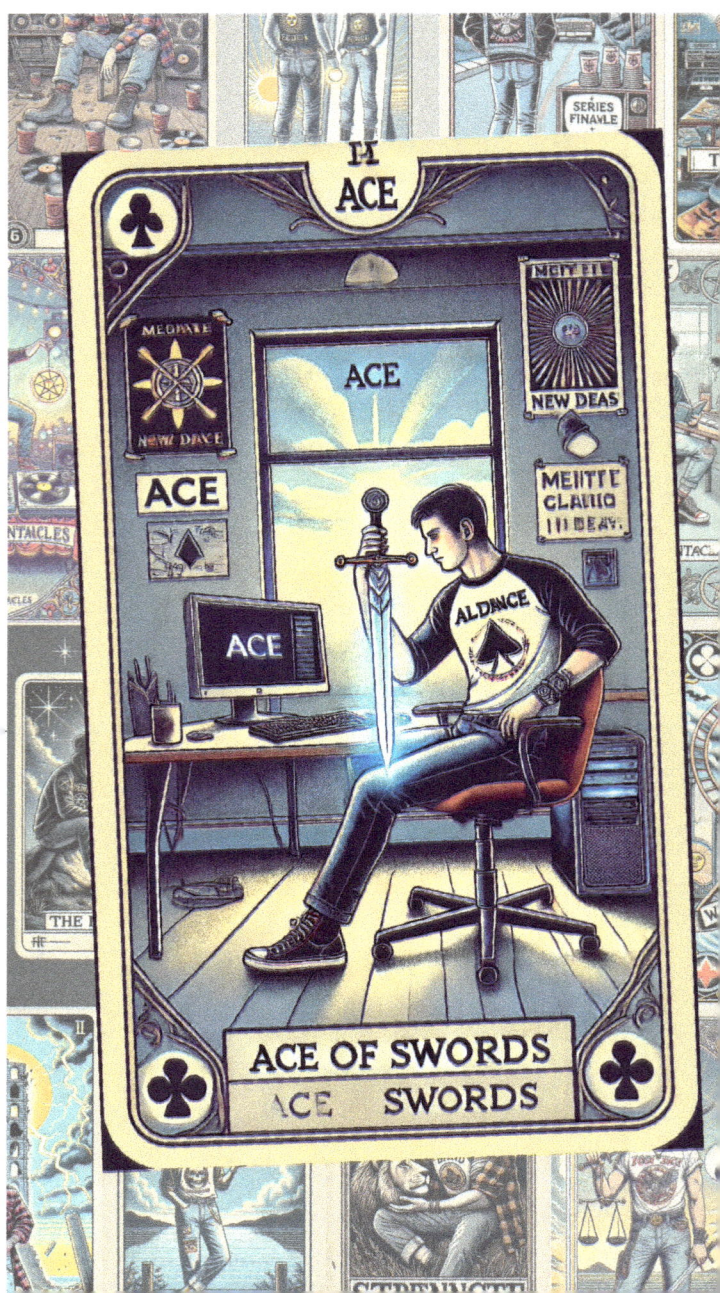

Ace of Swords

Clarity, new ideas, truth.

New clarity or idea. Cut through the BS and see things for what they are. Use your brain.

Quick take...

GO FOR IT!

See through the crap.

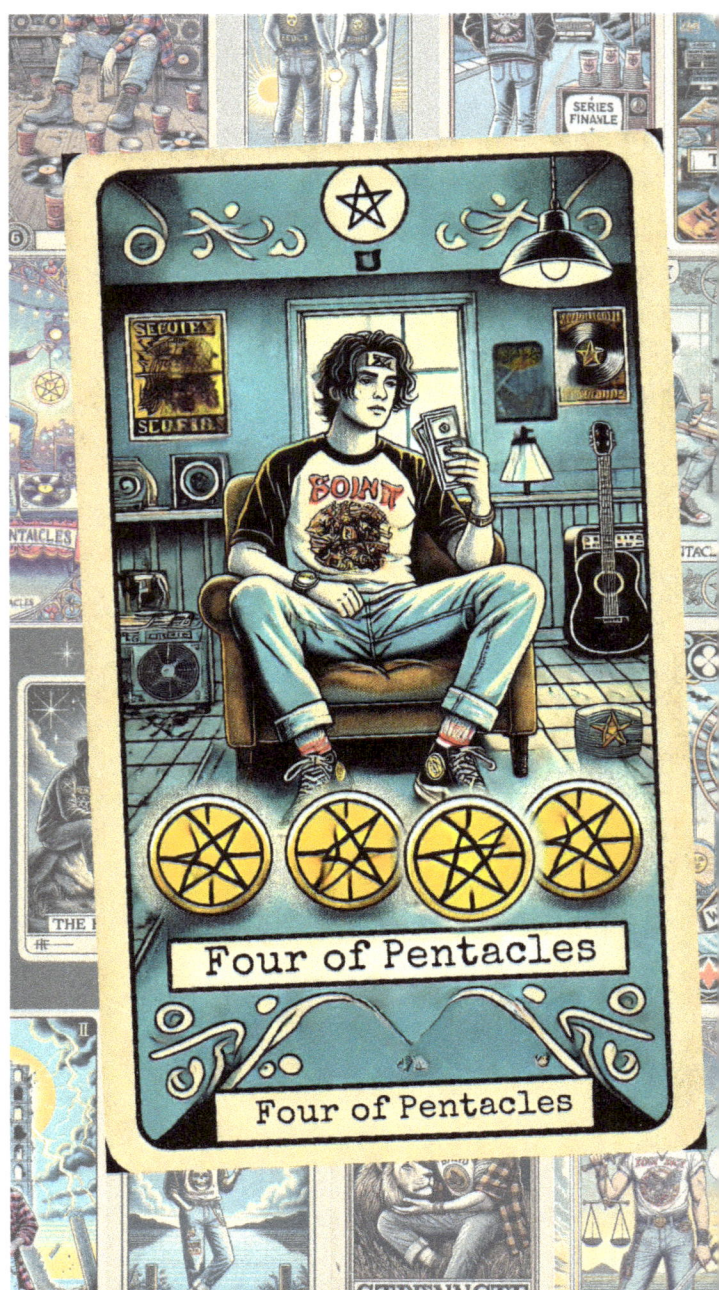

Four of Pentacles

Greed, control, possessiveness.

Holding on too tight? Relax your grip or miss out. Money ain't everything.

Quick take...
NOPE... NOT EVEN!

Loosen up, it's just cash.

Death

Transformation, endings, transition.

It's not the end, just a new beginning. Change is tough, but it's part of life. Deal with it.

Quick take...
YEP ... FOR SURE!
Endings are just new beginnings.

Ten of Wands

Burden, responsibility, stress.

Burdened and overwhelmed? Delegate or drop the dead weight. Don't carry it all yourself.

Quick take...

DON'T EVEN GO THERE!

Lighten the load.

Strength

Courage, strength, patience.

Suck it up and be strong. Inner strength beats brute force every time. Calm down and tackle problems head-on.

Quick take...

YEP ... FOR SURE!

Strength comes from within, chill out.

Page of Wands

Exploration, enthusiasm, discovery.

Excitement and new ideas. Embrace the adventure and be spontaneous. Life's an open road.

Quick take...

TOTALLY!

Embrace new adventures.

Queen of Cups

Compassion, care, sensitivity.

Emotional stability and nurturing. Take care of yourself and others. Compassion is key.

Quick take...

GO FOR IT!

Nurture with compassion.

Page of Swords

Curiosity, vigilance, communication.

New ideas? Share them. Curiosity and communication are your best friends.

Quick take...

GO FOR IT!

Curiosity fuels innovation.

Queen of Wands

Confidence, determination, vibrance.

Confidence and charisma. Own your power and inspire others. Lead with passion.

Quick take...

TOTALLY!

Lead with confidence.

Six of Swords

Transition, moving on, change.

Move away from the drama. Find smoother waters and leave the baggage behind.

Quick take...

GO FOR IT!

Leave the drama behind.

Queen of Swords

Independence, clarity, perception.

Cut through the nonsense with cold, hard truth. Be direct, even if it hurts.

Quick take...

GO FOR IT!

Truth over tact.

Three of Swords

Heartbreak, pain, loss.

Heartbreak sucks, but it's part of life. Deal with the pain and move on.

Quick take...
NOPE... NOT EVEN!
Pain is part of life.

Four of Swords

Rest, recovery, contemplation.

Take a break before you break. Rest and recuperate, you need it.

Quick take...
MEH ... WHATEVER!
Rest before you wreck yourself.

King of Cups

Balance, control, support.

Control your emotions with wisdom. Lead with a steady hand and a kind heart.

Quick take...

GO FOR IT!

Lead with a kind heart.

Six of Cups

Nostalgia, memories, childhood.

Nostalgia trip. Remember the good old days, but don't get stuck in the past. Keep moving forward.

Quick take...

I GUESS SO!?!

Remember, but don't get stuck.

Five of Pentacles

Poverty, insecurity, hardship.

Feeling left out in the cold? Suck it up and find a way in. Help is out there.

Quick take...

NOPE... NOT EVEN!

Help yourself by finding help.

Queen of Pentacles

Nurturing, practicality, security.

Nurture and care for your kingdom. Practicality and love go hand in hand.

Quick take...

YEP ... FOR SURE!

Care and practicality rule.

Six of Wands

Success, recognition, victory.

Victory and recognition. Bask in the glory but stay humble. Don't let it go to your head.

Quick take...

TOTALLY!

Enjoy the spotlight, stay humble.

King of Pentacles

Leadership, wisdom, success.

Boss mode. Lead with wisdom and ensure everyone's taken care of. Prosperity through leadership.

Quick take...

YEP ... FOR SURE!

Lead with wisdom and care.

The Emperor

Authority, structure, control.

Take charge and show 'em who's boss. Be assertive, but don't be a jerk about it. Stand your ground.

Quick take...

YEP ... FOR SURE!

Take charge without being a dictator.

Knight of Pentacles

Hard work, reliability, patience.

Slow and steady wins the race. Be reliable, even if it's boring.

Quick take...
MEH ... WHATEVER!
Dependability over speed.

Eight of Cups

Abandonment, withdrawal, journey.

Walking away? Sometimes you have to leave to find what you really want. It's not giving up, it's moving on.

Quick take...

DON'T EVEN GO THERE!

Leave to find better.

Three of Pentacles

Teamwork, collaboration, skill.

Teamwork makes the dream work, but only if everyone pulls their weight. Collaborate or crash.

Quick take...

GO FOR IT!

Work together or fail alone.

Nine of Pentacles

Success, luxury, reward.

Enjoy the fruits of your labor. You've earned it, so live it up.

Quick take...

GO FOR IT!

Enjoy your hard-earned success.

Four of Wands

Celebration, harmony, home.

Celebration and stability. Enjoy the moment and share the joy. Life's good.

Quick take...

TOTALLY!

Celebrate life's moments.

The Hanged Man

Suspension, letting go.

Sometimes you need to look at things from a different angle. Let go and see where it takes you.

Quick take...

I GUESS SO!?!

Look at it from another angle.

The Hierophant

Tradition, conformity, morality.

Traditions can be a drag, but sometimes you've gotta play by the rules to get ahead. Don't reinvent the wheel.

Quick take...

YEP ... FOR SURE!

Stick to the rules, even if they suck.

Six of Pentacles

Generosity, sharing, charity.

Give and take, man. What goes around comes around. Share your wealth.

Quick take...

GO FOR IT!

What goes around, comes around.

Knight of Swords

Ambition, haste, action.

Charge ahead, but watch where you're going. Reckless action leads to trouble.

Quick take...

MEH ... WHATEVER!

Look before you leap.

The Devil

Addiction, materialism, bondage.

Face your demons instead of running. Confront what's holding you back and break free from the chains.

Quick take...

AS IF ... NO WAY!

Face it, don't run away.

The Hermit

Introspection, solitude, guidance.

Take a step back and think things through. Alone time is golden, so embrace the solitude and find your way.

Quick take...

I GUESS SO!?!

Solitude is golden, embrace it.

Judgement

Judgment, rebirth, inner calling.

Own up to your actions and make amends. It's time to reflect and move forward with a clean slate.

Quick take...

I GUESS SO!?!

Reflect, own up, move on.

The World

Completion, accomplishment, travel.

You've made it, but don't get too comfy. Keep striving for more. Celebrate your achievements but keep moving.

Quick take...

YEP ... FOR SURE!

Celebrate, but keep striving.

Three of Cups

Celebration, friendship, joy.

Celebrate the good times. Life's too short not to party. Enjoy the moments with friends.

Quick take...

TOTALLY!

Party like there's no tomorrow.

JUST WRITE THAT CRAP DOWN...

JUST WRITE THAT CRAP DOWN...

JUST WRITE THAT CRAP DOWN...

JUST WRITE THAT CRAP DOWN...

… JUST WRITE THAT CRAP DOWN…

JUST WRITE THAT CRAP DOWN...

JUST WRITE THAT CRAP DOWN...

JUST WRITE THAT CRAP DOWN...

JUST WRITE THAT CRAP DOWN...

JUST WRITE THAT CRAP DOWN...

JUST WRITE THAT CRAP DOWN...

JUST WRITE THAT CRAP DOWN...

JUST WRITE THAT CRAP DOWN...

JUST WRITE THAT CRAP DOWN...

JUST WRITE THAT CRAP DOWN...

JUST WRITE THAT CRAP DOWN...

JUST WRITE THAT CRAP DOWN...

JUST WRITE THAT CRAP DOWN...

JUST WRITE THAT CRAP DOWN...

JUST WRITE THAT CRAP DOWN...

JUST WRITE THAT CRAP DOWN...

JUST WRITE THAT CRAP DOWN...

JUST WRITE THAT CRAP DOWN...

JUST WRITE THAT CRAP DOWN...

JUST WRITE THAT CRAP DOWN...

JUST WRITE THAT CRAP DOWN...

JUST WRITE THAT CRAP DOWN...

JUST WRITE THAT CRAP DOWN...

JUST WRITE THAT CRAP DOWN...

JUST WRITE THAT CRAP DOWN...

JUST WRITE THAT CRAP DOWN...

JUST WRITE THAT CRAP DOWN...

JUST WRITE THAT CRAP DOWN...

JUST WRITE THAT CRAP DOWN...

JUST WRITE THAT CRAP DOWN...

JUST WRITE THAT CRAP DOWN...

JUST WRITE THAT CRAP DOWN...

JUST WRITE THAT CRAP DOWN...

About the Author

Amanda Clarke is a spirited Gen X author renowned for her unorthodox approach to spirituality and tarot. Growing up in the vibrant chaos of the '80s and '90s, Amanda cultivated a unique blend of cultural nostalgia and mystical curiosity, qualities that now define her writings. Her latest book, "Flannel and Tarot Cards: A Gen Xer's Guide to Spiritual Insights," embodies her no-nonsense style, offering readers a refreshingly direct pathway to personal discovery and enlightenment. With a background in diverse spiritual practices and a penchant for raw, heartfelt advice, Amanda continues to inspire those seeking guidance without the mystical fluff.

The "Daily Guidance" series offers an innovative approach to finding spiritual wisdom and practical advice. Each book in the series is a unique tool designed for daily introspection and decision-making. Readers are invited to meditate on a question or seek general guidance for the day, then flip to a random page in the book. The page they land on provides a personalized message from various spiritual sources, such as angels, tarot, or spirit animals. With each turn of the page, these books deliver insightful, positive messages and mantras to inspire personal growth and provide clarity on life's daily challenges and decisions.

Other books in this series:-
The Crystal Pathway
The Angelic Oracles
Daily Angel Tarot Reading
Mystic Tarot Cat
Oracle of the Tarot Cat
Vibes Unveiled
Spirit Animal Oracle
Answers from the Oracles
Messages from the Angels

More on the Bookshelves at www.korupublishing.com

More on the Bookshelves at www.korupublishing.com